Head
of
The Willow

Head of The Willow

JUNE PENHELOG

The Cloister House Press

Copyright © 2024 June Penhelog

All rights reserved. No part of this publication may be reproduced or transmitted in any form or by any means, electronic or mechanical including photocopying, recording or any information storage or retrieval system, without prior permission in writing from the publishers.

The right of June Penhelog to be identified as the author of this work has been asserted by her in accordance with the Copyright, Designs and Patents Act 1988

First published in the United Kingdom in 2024 by
The Cloister House Press

ISBN 978-1-913460-81-5

Contents

The Blorenge	1
Home Deluxe	2
A Job Worth Doing	4
Chrysanthemums and Chickens	5
Miss Jones Takes Charge	6
The Rat Man Cometh	7
The Last Dance	8
To be a Somebody	9
Just Thinking	10
The Last Farewell	11
Hard Times	12
It Could Happen	13
Holding On	14
Woman in a Dressing Gown	16
Board Games and Talking	17
The Chapel Under the Hill	18
In My Care	19
A Child's Dream	20
Unwanted	21
The Rabbit	22
Growing Pains	23
Full Moon Experience	24
If I'd Known Him	25
Bottled Like Gucci	26
Mother	27
The Piano	28

Elegy for a Lost Uterus	29
Tell Me	30
The Willow and the Moon	31
Elegy for a Gypsy Child	32
The Memory Box	33
Speed Queen	34
Memories of Childhood	35
Accusing Finger	36
Foxtrot	37
The First Time	38
Perranarworthal	39
Mumbles	40
I Remember	41
The Wasp House	42
Memories of Kilvey Hill	43
Observation	44
The Promise	45
Leboyer Perhaps	46
Moving Out	47
Something New	48
Is That You?	49
Grandma Glowing's Beads	50
Look at the Sky	51
On Shingled Beach	52
Sweet Surrender	53
Dylan's Fuchsia	54
Abandoned	55
Aunty and Uncle Something	56
Free Range, Please	57

Lambs to the Slaughter	58
New Horizons	59
Not Far to the Beach	60
Part-time Lovers	61
The Hat	62

Inner peace begins the moment you choose not to allow another person or event to control your emotions.

The Blorenge

The Blorenge is a hill that overlooks the valley of the River Usk, near Abergavenny.

The discarded padded bra, carelessly thrown
on the bed, reminded me of the Blorenge.
I loved that mountain.
I've watched the sun, snow, and rain take
part in that dark vision.
The deep cleft, called the Punchbowl, collects
the shadows that play there.
A mountain of mystery is the Blorenge; it follows
you around. It will be watching whether you are
   strolling through Llanfoist
or walking through Abergavenny.
That is the sheer mystery of the Blorenge.

Home Deluxe

The box was big enough.
The writing on the side read
'Washing machine Deluxe'.
Just what I needed: a bit of Deluxe.

But the box wasn't available, not yet anyway.
It was being carried by a man dressed to kill.
He wore a smart suit with leather gloves and a trilby
tilted over one eye.

I could die for that box; I needed it badly. The weather
was turning cold, and I could feel it setting into my old
ankle fracture, causing a deep throb.

The toff stopped to look at me, probably not liking what
he saw. Well, I wouldn't like what he saw, either.
I was unwashed, with uncut hair and clothes matted to
   my body.
We parried glances: his look disdainful, I, well, hopeful.

'Excuse me,' I said. 'Is your box going into that skip?'
I almost said *sir* but managed to stop myself.
'It's a good size and would be just right for me.'
He continued to stare.
'I think we're in for snow tonight; the box would help
keep out the cold, if you know what I mean.'
He managed a wry smile and said he knew perfectly
   well
what I meant. He placed the box on the ground.
'It's all yours, son,' he said as he walked towards me.

He placed Home Deluxe at my feet. His smile deepened as he placed his leather-clad hand in mine.
'Keep warm, young man, and good luck.'
'Thank you,
Sir.'

A Job Worth Doing

'We need people like you,' he said,
'Someone who will work hard, always
punctual. You know, conscientious.'
I stood back so I could see his face.
He watched, eyeing my movement closely.

He wasn't a clean man, and I didn't like
what I saw. He ran the back of his hand
across his nose and sniffed, displaying a
remnant of mucous.

I turned away and studied the pile of pasties
stacked high in the window. The man reached
over and realigned a flaky item with a suspect finger.

'Well,' he said. 'Can I count you in?'
'No, sir,' I replied.
'I believe I'm allergic to pasties.'
The bell behind the shop door made a tinny
ring as I left.

Chrysanthemums and Chickens

We listened to the grown-ups talk about death,
about burying Bampy.
Bampy, who'd left the sea, came home to grow
Chrysanthemums and chickens and smoked
Woodbines.

Sometimes, he'd take us on the bus to Porthcawl,
So he could have a pint on the sly.
We didn't mind hiding his secret,
He was a good Bampy.

Now he's gone, and they are planning
his burial. We didn't like the sound of death.

The coffin had been placed on two chairs
In the front room, where friends would say goodbye.
A coffin in the front room!
We couldn't bear to think about that.

We couldn't bear to see a dead Bampy,
So, we went to bed early.

Miss Jones Takes Charge

Everything looked grey in that schoolyard,
with its uneven surface where you tripped
and grazed your knees.
But there was a tree in that yard, just one,
tall and bushy green.
One playtime, we stood around the tree and
watched and listened to the cries of a cat who
had climbed too high and was scared.
We called Miss Jones, we knew she would help,
she was the new art teacher.
She reached up and retrieved the screaming puss.
Then, she opened her brown leather shoulder bag
and took out a small suede brush and cleaned her shoes.
How easy it is to impress a young child.

The Rat Man Cometh

The rat man had been out on the prowl,
watching his new neighbour.
He didn't like her. Her voice was too nice;
and she had a dog.
When he walked past her, she smiled and
said good morning in her soft voice.
The sound of her riled him. He couldn't
put up with that; he'd teach her.

One day, he watched as she watered the potato plants
In her allotment, she was smiling to herself;
he couldn't allow her that pleasure.
So, that day, he set about his plan.
He found what he wanted on the riverbank: a juicy rat.
He caught it, killed it, disembowelled it, then spread the
evisceration over the flourishing potato plants.

That should take the smile off the posh bitch's face.

The Last Dance

The chicken danced in the garden,
he was big now and fluffy.
I held out my arms to him, offering
to be his partner.
His beak pecked at things, his eyes darted.
I loved to dance with Joey; he had once
    been a chicken.

Then, one day, just before Christmas,
I came home from school ready for
a dance, but Joey wasn't dancing,
he was hanging by his feet on the doornail,
    waiting to be plucked.

Gran said I shouldn't cry; Joey was getting
ready for Christmas.
    And it was time to grow up.

To be a Somebody

I used to be somebody with a big job, a big car, a big house, and an expensive family.
But when the job went out through the window, so did the family and friends.
Now, what am I?
I'll tell you what I am: I'm a nobody. A nobody waiting in a damp doorway for
handouts. A dirty, filthy mess of a man. The night is wet and cold; I shiver from
the pain of it all. I settle down in the doorway. My duvet, which hasn't heard
the sound of a washing machine since God knows when, is of little comfort,
but it's my comfort.
I hide beneath it, longing for food, waiting for a handout.
Waiting for the chance to be a somebody again.

Just Thinking

I often thought about being a vicar, a woman of the cloth.
I would stand in the pulpit and say good things.
I would smile benignly and pray.

I would have made a good vicar; my hair would
be clean and shiny, my nails smooth and pink.
I would hold hands with the parishioners and ask
if they were well. Occasionally, I would be all-pastoral
and visit those who were ailing.

But mostly, I would like to go into the vestry on my own,
sit in a vicar-type chair and drink deep red communion
wine out of a silver chalice.

The Last Farewell

I said goodbye to my ironing board today.
A new one was well overdue, but the old
one – how I hated to cast it aside.
I opened it up onto its wobbly legs, rusty
in places, but ready to talk.
It had come free with a washing machine,
years ago, when the kids were little.

The top cover was scorched and shredding,
hiding all the other covers: different faded
covers that told a tale.

The bottom layer would have ironed baby
clothes and husband number one's shirts.
Then, as the layers thickened, I saw shadows
of school clothes for you all, ironed with love.

Layer upon layer of memories: love, sadness, grief.
You have to go now, but some things want to hold
on, stay. I'm struggling, so I think I'll put you in the
shed. You can rest there, and I will pop in to see you
now and then.

Hard Times

I never thought it would get like this.
My cousin has just invaded my lovely
bedroom.
Mam said I have to be nice to her because
her dad's out of work and they
can't buy food. Well, we can't, either.
Food isn't like it used to be. Mam is
afraid to use the cooker; she can't afford it,
so, she has taken an extra job, and she's tired.
Dad hasn't worked since lockdown; it
was Covid that did it.
His lungs are bad, so he can't breathe.

Mam's taken in a lodger, though,
a big man from the building site,
he wears a tight T-shirt and spits.
The other day, when Mam was
upstairs, giving Dad his inhaler,
the dirty lodger grabbed me; he
pulled me onto his lap and breathed
against my throat. I felt sick from his smell.

I just want to be with Mam and Dad,
as it used to be before things changed,
before the food bank became our only
shop; before I felt ashamed.
When I was just Mam and Dad's girl.

It Could Happen

The floor is wet and cold,
seeping into my shabby clothes.
People rush around, glance down,
carry on with life.

My empty stomach contracts
as a reminder that food now
is a distant memory;
a memory of when I abused it.
Easy come, easy go.

This doorway affords some shelter,
protects me from rain, wind, abuse.
I still have my pride. I want to shout,
look at me – what do you see:
A filthy woman, a beggar?

No! No! A human being who was
once loved cared for. Who worked
for years caring for others.
So, look at me and remember:
It could happen to you.

Holding On

I dreaded going home today.
I dreaded the thought of telling
Annie, I had lost my job.
It would put paid to her; I knew it.

Her spirits are low, as it is,
following the baby coming early.
Well, it messed things up a bit;
not that she could help.

I had warned her often enough,
not that she would listen.
She had to keep doing things,
even in her state.
Save a bit here, save a bit there.

I knew I'd be out first. I'd only been
there a month, so, last in, first out.
What the fuck could I do?
Sign on again; no bloody choice.

The rent went up again last month,
I had a word with the landlord, of course,
but I knew he wouldn't be bothered.
His wife wouldn't be crying because
the pantry was empty.

Annie barely had enough money to
buy the baby nappies and herself pads.
One night, I thought it might be easier
for her if I wasn't around anymore.
Yes, my thoughts were becoming pretty
dark. Poor Annie wouldn't like that.

She was lying next to me in the bed we'd
bought last year in the Ikea sale, her breathing
soft and trusting. The little one was in his crib,
making soft baby sounds. So lovely to hear.

Could I leave this?
Give it all up?
Please, God, no.
LET ME HOLD ON.

Woman in a Dressing Gown

Dark morning street where gravel
crunches. A tear-filled Kleenex drops,
to be destroyed by damp air.

Pulling her dressing gown around
her skeletal frame, she weeps again,
weeps for herself, for others;
for the child who never grew.

The belt of her dressing gown
trails in a collection of yesterdays;
she tucks the filthy end into her pocket,
hiding shame.

She drifts on, wanting to care,
trying to recall the memories,
but they're beyond reach.
Don't struggle –
let them lie dormant.

Board Games and Talking

I used to love baking,
heating up the oven,
making things;
but I can't anymore.

We used to sit together
and watch Sky or Netflix;
but that's all gone.

Sometimes I'd buy fish
and chips, once in a while;
but I can't anymore.

So, we have to settle for
for other things, like
board games and talking.

Yes, we've begun to
enjoy that again:
board games and talking.

The Chapel Under the Hill

I loved that chapel on the corner under the hill.
It was old and dark; well, the back was dark,
the front was lovely.
I loved the inside of that chapel;
the pulpit was large and shining;
the candlesticks glowed,
the velvet drapes swayed.

The hymn numbers hung on the wall,
at the side of the pulpit.
I liked guessing which hymn would
be sung first in the service.
The organist would pedal like fury,
looking into the mirror to see if
Miss Frobisher, whom he fancied,
was there. Of course, he knew she
she was there, he'd have recognized
that soprano voice, anywhere.

As I've said, the back of the chapel
was dark and home to bats and rats.
Mam said bats would stick in your hair,
and you'd have to be shaved bald.
The rats were evil, too; they'd been
known to kill babies in cots, well,
that's what Mam said.

But I loved that chapel.
I was baptized there.
I was married there.
Mam's funeral was there.
Yes, I loved that chapel under the hill.

In My Care

You were the worst kind of bully,
making fun of the way
I spoke, hurting me.
You were the leader of the
gang, the main one.
I vowed that one day, it would
be payback time.

Many years later, you came
Into the labour ward, having
your first baby. Your waters
had broken. You were panting,
crying.
I said, 'Hello, I'm your midwife,
I will deliver your baby.'
Pulling on a pair of surgical
gloves, I prepared to examine you.

'Don't worry,' I said,
'you'll be fine.'
You looked at me,
eyes pleading.
Sorry, sorry, they said.

Well, we all grow up, don't we?

A Child's Dream

I wanted a garden swing.
I wanted to be pushed high,
So the feeling in my stomach
would make me laugh.

But we didn't have a swing,
because we didn't have a garden
and we didn't have a house.

The people we lived with,
Aunty something, didn't want
us there, so I was unhappy.

One day, when I'm grown up
and clever, I'll buy a house; it
will be clean and warm and
we'll have food with some chicken.
And a swing in the garden.

Unwanted

You were given a chance,
a chance to live.
For twelve weeks, you floated
in a well of amniotic fluid:
fluid to sustain you.

Your life, dear one, wasn't required;
you had no part to play,
a mere hindrance;
surplus to requirements.

I remember holding the metal
kidney dish, in which you lay.
Your body supine, an offering
beneath bright arc lights;
your final resting place.

Your beauty was beyond belief.
Eyelids etched in blue:
as blue as the veins that
glowed through your gentle skin.
Yes, dear one, sweet, fragile life.
I remember you.

The Rabbit

I remember the first time
we made love,
we'd borrowed a room from
your friend.
You removed my top, and I
introduced you to the Rabbit.

He was a special tattoo on
my stomach. You said you loved
that rabbit. You loved his smile.

Later, when I became pregnant
with the twins, the Rabbit's face
changed, took on a different look,
but still smiled.

After the twins were born, you
complained and said the Rabbit had
changed. My loose stomach
had made his smile slack and ugly.

Poor Rabbit, poor me ...

Growing Pains

Gathering wood chippings from the sawmills,
gathering cinders from the railway yard,
getting soaked to the skin;
is character-building.

Scrubbing the steps,
sweeping the paths,
beating the mats.
That's character-building.

Going to chapel,
singing the hymns,
watching the offerings
fall into the basket.
It's character-building.

Hearing about Dad.
Lost at sea.
Seeing Mam cry,
just you and me.
All character-building.

Full Moon Experience

Last night, when the moon was full,
I needed to be naked. I wanted the soft
rays to graze my body.
I looked up at the face; I outlined
the eye and mouth with my finger.
It was a real face; anyone could see that.
A light breeze lifted my hair, so I caught a
strand and sucked it slowly.
Then I felt your fingers caress my shoulders
as you slipped my dress onto the damp grass
where we lay. Where you took possession,
instructed by me.

If I'd Known Him

If my father hadn't died
before I knew him,
If he'd lived long enough
for me to say hello,
He would have taught
me things and told me
about the sea and life
perhaps.
If he hadn't died, he might
have liked my hair and thought
me pretty. He would have held
my hand.
If my father hadn't died, he would
have taught me to swim and
remember things, like the names
of plants and sea creatures.
But, most of all, I would have
loved to have heard his voice,
rough, perhaps from all the salty
sea. I'm thinking about what it
would have been like if I had known
my father.

Bottled like Gucci

Vernix caseosa is the name given to the creamy substance that protects the baby whilst in utero.

Sweet head that nestled into my hands,
how I love the feel of you: Your warmth,
your shape, your perfect covering of *vernix caseosa*. A beauty product no cosmetic magnate could replicate.
Your body shrouded in a soft light coating of white cream, with a scent that will linger in my mind forever.
I bend over your small body; I inhale your amazing newborn smell and wish it could be bottled like *Gucci*.

Mother

*This poem is in memory of a mother who loved me
but no longer knew me.*

Do you know my daughter?
Do you know her name?
You really are quite like her,
your eyes are just the same.

She's usually here quite early
to take me for my treat,
but I don't mind waiting with you,
I'm so glad that we should meet.

I wish you'd met my daughter,
we always have such fun;
she buys me glasses of vino,
and laughs at things we've done.

I'm waiting for my daughter,
but I'd like to know your name;
you really are so like her,
I'm very glad you came.

The Piano

I lied.
I couldn't help it.
I had nothing to show you.
I was ashamed of how I was.
How I lived.

You had so much,
So, I pretended.

I have a piano;
my mother bought it
after my father died.
It's in the front room.
I can play.
I'm having lessons.

You just looked at me.
I could tell you didn't
believe me.
It was nice of you
to pretend, though.

I'm grown up now.
I have a piano,
and I can play.

Elegy for a Lost Uterus

I lost my uterus today.
I cried.
My precious child-bearing organ
has been removed from its
warm place.

I never thought I'd lose you,
you worked so hard for me:
cuddled and cocooned my little ones,
sustained them.

I feel an emptiness in the space
where once you lay.
A part of me, who I used to be,
has gone – and I'm sad.

Tell Me

Tell me, please.
Tell me how you feel when you look at me.
Am I so very different from the girl you met
all those years ago? Do you still feel that *zing* when
you touch me?

Are my eyes just as blue, and does your pulse
still race when I purr and stroke you?
I hope so.
You see, I think about it often, too often,
it seems.

I look at you and still love what I see.
I love your touch, that special something
that makes me tingle in places.
Have I changed so much, be honest, please.

No! No! I've changed my mind.
Don't say a word ...

The Willow and the Moon

The willow was dipping low,
brushing my face; I liked that.
It was as if the tree enjoyed my presence.

The moon shone through the boughs,
as if they knew each other.
I think they did.

I found a space in the night
beneath the willow and the Moon.
Pressing my back against her strength,
I felt at peace.

Peace at last within me.
I will become part of the willow.
The Moon will watch.

Elegy for a Gypsy Child

Your tangled hair is spread
over the pillow,
skin marbled white,
eyes closed, at peace now.
A beautiful gypsy child.
Your name is Estelle.
Star.
I brushed your lovely black hair,
you didn't wince.
I dressed you in your best dress,
I stroked your lips,
I whispered a prayer.
You're free now, sweet Estelle:
The brightest star of all.

The Memory Box

We were lovers long before we married.
The feeling had sprung up between us, biting
with a deep passion.
The first time you drove me home, I dropped
my gloves in your car, knowing you'd find them.
I had to work fast, I wanted you badly.
I got you.
We shared so many years together, difficult,
times; destructive times.
Now I look at you lying beside me, the silver-
blue scar on your chest that saved your life
reminds me that I still love you: your voice,
your hands, your name, which will always be mine.

A selection of memories stored in a box with a pair of
gloves.

Speed Queen

Pulsating through the revs.
Accelerator pedal to metal.
Aircon blowing.
Music pulsating.
Skirt above thighs;
rise high, go on.
Speed!

You okay, Thelma?
Just fine, Louise.
Getting pissed when I stop this baby.
You going to stop, Louise?
Yes, but speed exhilarates.
Okay, okay! Yes, speed is so good.
It's done great things for me, remember?
Don't start boasting again.

So where next, Thelma?
Supermarket, of course,
I'm running out of wine.
Ha! Ha! Ha!
Bitch!

Memories of Childhood

The child was lifted onto the tall
plastic chair. So cold against her
mottled, malnourished skin.
The nurse tied a cold rubber cape around
the girl's neck, pinching her.

Pushing the child's head forward, the nurse
inspected the mass of pale blonde hair:
tangled and filthy. The girl cried, tears
streaming down her face. The nurse tut-tutted
at what she saw. *Lousy child*.

With a practiced hand, the nurse grabbed
a pair of scissors and started hacking at the hair,
allowing it to fall in a blonde mass around the chair.
Then she reached for the razor; yes, this will do
the job. The child sobbed, hoping for pity; none came.

Hair stuck to the tears and snot, lice drowning in the
salty mucous. The last of the hair fell before her, and the
scraping of the razor stopped. She was bald.
The nurse helped her off the chair, kinder now.
The girl raised her hands to touch the spiky baldness.
'Don't worry, dear; it could grow back curly.'

Accusing Finger

So many times, I have stood in this place.
I've gazed at the dark skeletal form:
wild, menacing, beckoning.
The tall line of the chimney
points skyward: an accusing finger.
At its worst, the sea will lash
and beat against your experienced stone.
The stones that know so much
have seen so much:
laughter, crying, pain.

Man working, man living, man dying.
But you have crumbled now,
lost your strength and power.
You've crumbled into the sea and
settled on the cliffs.
Now you are invaded, tormented;
no rest for you, old man.
The crowds come from far and wide.
screeching like a flock of gulls.
They look at your remains; they gasp in wonder.

But I'd like them to have known you,
to have seen you and your strength,
as you were in a day long gone:
mighty, powerful!
A giant amongst men; a Cornish Tin Mine ...

Foxtrot

The fox trotted over
the green; stopped,
licked his paw,
sniffed the ground
and moved on.

He blinked against the
sun's brightness,
pawed the cool air,
moved on again
in a haze of red.

The First Time

The first time I saw a dead body, I cried.
It was so still, with a colour difficult to
describe; waxen, perhaps.
I was asked to wash and dress the body
to make her look as she had always looked.
Yes, it was *she*. A woman with a name: Annie.
Now, she was in my care.
I filled a bowl with warm, scented water
and, with a soft cloth, began washing her pale skin.
I combed her hair gently, but it still caught a tangle;
she didn't complain, didn't say *ouch*.
She'll never complain again.
I washed her breasts and imagined her feeding
her baby, holding it close, experiencing that feeling
peculiar to women. Soft warmth, uterus contracting,
as the milk gently flowed over her little one's lips.
So much pride, so much love.

Thank you for allowing me time with you, Annie;
I will never forget.

Perranarworthal

A small Cornish village, between Truro and Falmouth

The cottage faced the sea,
morning mist would lift to
show the beauty ahead.
Seagulls accompanied the
start of day, making it real.

Such blueness, power, and promise,
but I like the afternoon when
the Cornish mist will crawl
up the garden to greet me;
and settle me down for the night.

Mumbles

Walking the beach near the pier,
dresses tucked into knickers,
hankies over our heads.

Finding rockpools
that hold excitement.
Winkles perhaps?

A plastic bucket,
rough around the edges,
will hold our treasures.
A present for Mother.

Sand sticks to our toes,
covers our feet;
a lovely feeling of belonging.
Belonging to the sea.

Two little mermaids
having fun.
Listen to the waves!
Feel the peace.
Enjoy being a child again.

I Remember

I remember when you left,
it was a Wednesday.
I drove you to the station,
kids screaming.

You got out with your suitcase,
you stood on the kerb.
I think you took a mental
photo of us and the dented car.

You caught the train to London,
then on to Australia.
She was with you,
a form of comfort.

You only called when you
needed to say how happy
you were without me – us.
I thought of you, though.

You sent me a boomerang for
Christmas. Boasting again,
you in the sun, me and the kids
shivering.

The Wasp House

The apples you bought
today were lovely,
except for one, it was
occupied by a wasp.
He was making a home:
hollowing out the fruit.
A wonderful job he made, too.
Then he called in his friends.
They took possession.

Memories of Kilvey Hill

Even the docks looked lovely
from the top of Kilvey Hill.
The sea salt grey.
Shadows of ships;
a soft horizon.

Everything looked lovely
from Kilvey Hill.
Looking over a piece of Swansea,
a small piece that told a tale.

Ghosts moved off the docks
from Kilvey Hill.
Ghosts of my childhood,
ghosts just waiting to scare.

Not much of a hill is Kilvey Hill,
green in places, plus the stones.
But adventures were made,
and growing up planned,
on Kilvey Hill.

Observation

My father takes me places.
He has artificial hips.
You'd be surprised what he can
do now.
After the operation, he was in
a wheelchair,
then he had physio and could
manage slow walks.
I don't like slow,
I'm not used to it.
Father said that sometimes
slow is good, you can see things
you'll miss when you rush.
You'll hear wonderful sounds, too.
My father was right.

The Promise

I shall build you a house,
somewhere in France.
When you visit,
we will become lovers.

I shall go to bed before
you and pretend to sleep.
You will wear stiletto heels,
which will sound lovely
on the stone steps.

I shall be listening.

Leboyer Perhaps

Frédérick Leboyer was a French obstetrician and is best known
for his 1974 book, *Birth Without Violence*.
Birth from an infant's point of view.

Try the Leyboyer method, suggested my friend;
you love it. No shouting, no banging of instruments;
just soft music of your choice and a kind, smiling
   midwife.
What an experience; I loved it.

It seemed too good to be true.
That evening, I sorted out my collection
of DVDs. Hmm, Chopin might help, or Stevie Wonder,
   even.
I felt excited. I only had two weeks to go, so with
   everything
remaining normal, I should be fine. I'll have a word
   with my midwife.

The next day, whilst walking through Tesco, amongst
   the baked
beans and spaghetti hoops, my waters broke.
The manager's office wasn't too uncomfortable,
but the music was crap.

Moving Out

When Friday came, he had gone,
packed his belongings, plus some of mine,
such as the penguin he'd bought last year
when I'd told him I was pregnant.
I loved that penguin.

Things he didn't want, he threw against
the wall: old socks, dirty socks, and
the scan photo of our foetus at twelve
weeks. Our little one, who
had fallen from life. He couldn't tolerate
my grieving.

So, he'd decided to move on.
Try again.
Some other place.
Some other woman perhaps.

Something New

You brought her into our home.
It was late, I heard you.
The kids slept.

You probably plied her with
our drink and pawed her.
Very you.

You had just bumped into her.
You said she'd looked amazing:
perfect makeup,
wonderful eyes.

Why didn't I do something
with myself? you asked.
Try a little harder,
you're not bad-looking, really.

'Hang on a moment, love,
 I'll run it past the kids.
You know, our kids;
all four of them are upstairs playing.'

Is That You?

Is that you calling,
Is that your voice I hear?
I wish it could be,
but it isn't.

Is that you rustling the newspaper,
turning each page with care?
It sounds like you,
but it isn't.

Is that your footstep I hear,
crunching on the garden path,
walking towards the door,
calling my name, already smiling?
It should be you,
but it isn't.

Grandma Glowing's Beads

So lovely the beads
that hung from her throat:
iridescent, glowing,
catching the light,
light of her dreams.
Piercing, strong,
revealing the woman,
she is not the woman
she was.
She waits, she watches;
looks into your eyes.
Don't be fooled.
Don't go near;
she's waiting.
Keep away,
her moves are precise,
practised. Take care, she's
ready, reaching out.
Grandma Glowing …

Look at the Sky

It was Sunday afternoon when I
realized what I had to do.
I gathered the children from
the parlour,
then in crocodile fashion
we ventured to the sea.

The sand that day was cool,
accepting our feet with a kind
of love. As we approached the
small waves, I stretched out
my arms, gathering you around me.

Look at the sky, I murmured.
The sun is leaving us, but the
Moon is waiting for our last farewell.
We will always remember this day.

On Shingled Beach

The lazy sound of the sea
on Shingled Beach welcomed me.
I loved this place; it was always
here for me.

The shingle folded over my feet,
the sharp bits abusing the soft skin.
Soon gentle white sand would
caress me as they sank into its warmth.

I loved how the pressure of my feet
allowed mini pools to form,
revealing gentle creatures of the sea.

Sometimes, I would kneel down
to investigate my treasures before
seeking the waves at the water's edge.

Sweet Surrender

The wind tapped on my window
and said he was frightened of the dark.
The noise was hollow that night,
whistling through the eves.

I wished the wind would become silent,
as silent as the moon.
The moon was silver that night,
with a face anyone would recognize.

The wind reminded me of his fear,
as if I didn't care.
I was there, wasn't I, listening.
I returned to my bed.
I preferred the moon.

Dylan's Fuchsia

A dried-out
withered fuchsia
sits within the pages
of my Dylan Thomas
collection.

I can see you standing
there, sweet-smelling
flowers behind your
back.
A thing men do.

Abandoned

The railway station was damp,
people pushed and dodged,
darted around me;
not caring.
I waited for you.
You would step down from the train,
smiling, reaching out to me.
Nearly time.
I glanced at the clock,
pulse racing.
You'll soon be here,
people surged forward.

I watched as the train drew near;
it stopped, and people jumped
onto the platform;
some smiling.
There you were!
Looking ahead, eager,
arms outstretched.
I moved towards you
then I realized your smile
 wasn't directed at me.
You grabbed her, whoever she was,
kissed her, wheeled her around;
laughing.

Aunty and Uncle Something

When the others moved out, they came to stay in our
 house.
The man, Uncle Something, had lost a leg, so he
 struggled.
The Aunty Something was bossy and unkind.
If she wanted to be mean, she would hide the artificial
 limb
and cause havoc.

They shouldn't have been there, really, but they had lost
 their house
after the accident. Mam said they could stay because
 they could
pay rent, and the extra money would buy food.

Bit by bit, we were losing our home to strangers, and I
 felt ashamed,
so, I lied. I pretended our home was lovely and that we
 had a big
 garden and chicken on Sundays with gravy and bread.
And one day, it would all come true.

Free Range, Please

Today has been a lovely day.
I met a fox in the meadow,
A beautiful creature he was, too.
As a special treat, I threw him a
piece of chicken.
He looked at me, almost smiling,
well, it was free range.
Then, he turned away and vanished,
In a haze of red.

Lambs to the Slaughter

Excuse me, are you from around here?
I'm looking to go on a nice walk.
You know, somewhere only locals know.
Somewhere with beauty, trees, atmosphere,
but nowhere too difficult; I'm no expert.
I need to think things over.
Sort things out.
Focus.
I have a problem, but I think I can be brave here.
It's to do with a guy. He's a physical person.
He hits me.
You're a stranger but the only one who knows about this.
Strange how I can open up to you when you don't know me.
The man pulled up his collar,
turning away, sheepish.
Sorry, I didn't mean to bother you.
This walk will help,
will give me strength from his fists.
Thank you for listening.
As the man turned, I saw the purple bruising on his neck.
I read his pain.

Not sheepish at all.
Just another lamb to the slaughter.

New Horizons

A long, snowy waste of time to a new place.
Windscreen wipers heavy with ice, shivering bodies
waiting for comfort.
White frozen hedgerows, erect, hiding their ferocity.
Never-ending roads, ice sculpted in spikes besides
   ghostly barns
dressed in white, as pure as any bride.

The complaining car struggles for purchase on the
   disfigured road
that can take us to an unfamiliar home.
I shiver into my coat. Painfully cold fingers, painful
   breasts,
the object of preparation for the little one who sleeps
   within me.
Waiting to be part of a new way of life, a new way of
   being,
              It has to work.

Not Far to the Beach

In the Moggy Thou, the picnic is packed
with wellies and macs.
Drive towards the wonderful sea; it's
waiting.

Our favourite spot is close to the rocks,
rocks shaped like chairs and even a table,
all ready for our picnic.

Look at the sea, pure Swansea Bay blue,
just waiting for our screams when icy water
attacks our toes.
Tablecloth spread over our rock table, but
collecting sand anyway. Doesn't sand taste great
with cheese and memories?

Part-time Lovers

The Pullman train slowed
at the junction.
I looked in at them,
sitting in a spot of luxury.

Some smiled, kissed,
gazed lovingly.
A glass of champagne
was raised.
Look at us, they said.
We love each other.

For now, anyway.

The Hat

You liked to wear a trilby hat,
a James Cagney lookalike, you said.
You wore it at an angle, dipped towards
your left side, your side of preference.
Vain, as ever.

It suited you, though:
I thought you looked handsome.
But when you left me for a newer model,
you left your hat behind;
a good idea, too.

Now it's my turn to wear the hat:
dipped to one side; posing.
Greta Garbo perhaps.

Milton Keynes UK
Ingram Content Group UK Ltd.
UKHW030649240724
446081UK00004B/263